CAN I *REALLY* AFFORD IT?

A Guide on How to Budget
& "Live Within Your Means"

Nancy Marie Barnes, Ph.D.

CAN I *REALLY* AFFORD IT?

A Guide on How to Budget
& "Live Within Your Means"

Publisher: CreateSpace Publishers, Scott's Valley, CA, part of the Amazon group of companies. An Amazon.Com. Company All rights reserved.

ISBN: 1440490678
EAN-13: 9781440490675.

Author: Nancy Marie Barnes, Ph.D.
Editing: James A. Barnes, Jr., Ph.D.
Cover design: Nancy Marie Barnes, Ph.D. using Cover Creator

Printed in the United States of America by CreateSpace Publishers, 100 Enterprise Way, Suite A200, Scott's Valley, CA, 95066, USA.

Bulk purchases, please contact nbarnes@dishmail.net or CreateSpace Publishers.

DEDICATION

This book is dedicated to my supportive, creative, caring, bright, analytical, loving, and wonderful husband Jim---my best friend and muse, with special appreciation for his editorial comments and contributions.

This book is also dedicated to my parents. They gave me confidence, Christian values, memories of wonderful family traditions, and an abundance of love and support.

And of course, this book is dedicated to my memorable, wise and inspiring grandparents, great-grandparents, and wonderful relatives, but especially my sister Linda, and my two brothers Richard and John.

About the author . . .

Dr. Nancy Marie Barnes

A native of California, Nancy Marie Barnes graduated from college with a BA and then obtained her Master's degree (M.A.) and Doctorate (Ph.D.).

Throughout her administrative/professional career, she utilized her writing skills, publishing various literary works. In addition, she simultaneously has been writing novels, poetry, nonfiction, screenplays, and web sites.

The concept of "service to others" is her motto. Thus, this book is dedicated to sharing with and helping others . . . in assisting interested persons, young and old, in being the best they can be.

This book is dedicated to you, its reader.

FOREWORD

This book was written for anyone in need of additional assistance in doing a family budget, managing one's finances and "living within their means."

With over 30 years of budgeting and management experience, both personally and in management positions, including almost 20 years as a CEO, this book was written for the specific purpose of helping interested persons learn more about the "budgeting process" and managing one's finances, including helpful strategies to "live within one's means."

This book was written reflecting the author's personal experience and opinions as to what constitutes a "good" family budget and how to "live within one's means."

The goal of this book is to help interested persons be successful and, therefore, affect their entire lives and sense of financial well-being---to be successful in managing personal finances and plan for a comfortable, stable future!

Good Budgeting!

TABLE OF CONTENTS

CAN I *REALLY* AFFORD IT?

A Guide on How to Budget
& "Live Within Your Means"

INTRODUCTION

You see something you *REALLY* like and you automatically reach for that old credit card. You ALWAYS use the card. Right? Everyday. Everywhere. You see something and you just get it. Why not!?! Good move? Maybe not.

Do you know if you can REALLY afford it?

EVERY time you reach for that card, you need to ask yourself four questions:

1. *"Can I afford it?"*

2. *Does it fit into my budget?*

3. *Do I even have a written monthly budget?*

4. *Does my budget allow for the purchase I want to make . . . in cash?*

In other words, do you know how to "live within your means"? Or put another way . . . do you know what that REALLY means?
Read on . . .

If you cannot fully answer any one of these questions, you may benefit significantly by re-thinking your finances.

Many people have found themselves in financial trouble because they didn't *REALLY* have a budget . . . What they called "their budget" was grossly incomplete or unrealistic.

Many people have found themselves in financial trouble because they were not "living within their means."

If this be true for you . . . then read this entire book, make out a written budget that reflects the budget elements in this book and your special needs and situation . . . and then follow it and "live within your means."

LIVING WITHIN YOUR MEANS

"Living within your means" enables you to if remain solvent, being ready for a "rainy day," and meeting your future needs.

You NEED to have your "assets" (income) in excess of your liabilities (bills and expenses). You need to be able to pay your debts and have money left over each month to place in your savings account for future emergencies and major expected expenses.

For sure, your goal or objective should be to be solvent, financially sound, debt-free, creditworthy, solid, secure, and "in the black" with a balanced retirement portfolio.

You have an obligation to your family and yourself to live within your means.

The purpose of this book is to help you live within your means, to feel successful and to be pleased with yourself and your finances.

Read through this entire book. Make copies of the budget chart. Fill it out. Analyze your financial situation. Then live within your means! Be financially proactive!

BUDGET PRIORITIES

WHAT you spend your money on each month, tells us what your priorities actually are . . . not what you **say** they are, but what they **really** are. Where are your priorities?

Make a check mark in front of each item that you spent money on in recent weeks. Then analyze your expenditures.

_____ Groceries

_____ Starbucks or coffee take-out

_____ Mortgage or rent payment

_____ Designer clothing

_____ Vacation

_____ Dental needs

_____ Home, state, federal taxes

_____ Extra pair of expensive, brand-name sports shoes

_____ CD's, DVD's, etc.

_____ Eating out

_____ Fancy expensive sports car (extra payment costs)

_____ Manicure or pedicure

_____ Utilities bill(s)

_____ New video or electronic equipment

_____ Deposit(s) into Saving Account

_____ Jewelry

_____ Gas (to go work)

_____ CD's, DVD's, etc.

_____ Investments

_____ Sports club membership fees

_____ Insurance (Car, home, medical, life, etc.)

_____ Other items (list)

Now, let's analyze this same list in another way. What were actual necessities (basic living items) and what could be considered non-necessities (you can live without them)?

NECESSITIES:

_____ Groceries

_____ Mortgage or rent payment

_____ Utilities bill(s)

_____ Auto loan payment

_____ Gas (to go work)

_____ Dental needs

_____ Home, state, federal taxes

_____ Auto loan payment

_____ Investment(s)

_____ Deposit(s) into Saving Account

NON-NECESSITIES:

_____Starbucks or coffee take-out

_____ Fancy expensive sports car (extra payment costs)

_____ Extra pair of expensive, brand-name sports shoes

_____ Eating out

_____ Vacation

_____ Manicure or pedicure

_____ Designer clothing

_____ New video or electronic equipment

_____ Jewelry

_____ Sports club membership fees

_____ Insurance (Car, home, medical, life, etc.)

Add other items to the list, reflecting any other expenses. Try to remember *all* your expenses and list them.

Those WERE your financial priorities. What SHOULD they have been? If they are one and the same, then you have done well. If you paid for all the "Necessities" then you have done well. Are these what you *REALLY* can afford?   If not, then you may need to re-think your priorities.

"GROSS" VS "NET" INCOME

To plan a budget, you need to know your "net" income which is what you have left after everything is taken out of your check---your "take home pay."

If you get paid by check, look at your check stub. Find the amount that you get paid **BEFORE** anything is deducted or taken out of your check. That is your **"gross" income** amount.

As you probably know there will be several required deductions from your "gross" or total salary amount. These typically are automatic deductions from your check. You never see the money.

Your check stub will list all your deductions or money taken out of your check (for example, state and federal taxes, Social Security, Medicare, unemployment insurance, medical insurance premium contribution, union dues, etc.). These are all subtracted from your "gross" salary or income. Some people have upwards to 30% of their gross check allocated out . . . leaving about 70% left. What is left is your **"net" income** or "take-home" pay, to pay your bills and provide for your day-to-day expenses.

Whether you are paid weekly or every two weeks, calculate your *monthly* net income. By doing so, you will be able to compare your monthly income with your monthly expenses.

If you get paid once a week: To arrive at your monthly net income, multiply your weekly net income by four (4), or 4.5, as some people do it, for four and a half weeks (as there are actually 4 and a half weeks in a full month).

If you get paid every two weeks (biweekly): To arrive at your monthly net income, multiply your biweekly net pay by 2.25 for your monthly net income.

If you get paid by the month, no calculation is necessary.

Now you need to look at your monthly expenses.

ANALYZING ONE'S
INCOME & EXPENSES

With your monthly income in mind, you are ready to analyze your income and expenses.

Make a copy of the budget chart provided for your convenience in this chapter, fill it out, and then analyze your financial situation. Cost out *ALL* your monthly expenses. No fudging! Be honest with yourself. List them all, without exception, if that item applies to you. (Not everyone has, for example, Association Fees. Leave that blank.)

If you pay something once a year, then divide that amount by 12 [months] and write in that amount. And no guessing. Use exact costs.

At the end of the budget chart, you will subtract your total monthly expenses from your monthly income. Then we'll talk about the difference.

Ideally, you should invest 10% of your gross income (before you even see your paycheck). If you are not already in a 401k or 403(b) retirement plan, you need to sincerely consider investing 10% or more into no-load, low-cost mutual funds, such as Vanguard. (If you can't invest 10% or to the maximum allowable by law, it's important to invest *something*, even 1% or 2.5% or 5%. Just do *something*.) In doing so, you paying yourself first and foremost for your future retirement years.

Ideally, your monthly expenses are less than your monthly income. Ideally, you have money left over each month. We'll see . . . let's go

MY MONTHLY BUDGET

DATE:_____

GROSS MONTHLY INCOME	Budget Item Costs	MONTHLY EXPENSE	INCOME MINUS EXPENSES
	Home Mortgage or Rent		
	Home/Renters Insurance		
	Home & Land Taxes		
	Investments (10% of gross income)		
	Credit Card(s) Payment(s)		
	Credit Card(s) Total Owed		
	Garbage Services		
	Utilities (Gas & Lights)		
	Water Bill		
	Association Fees (if any)		
	Home Phone (Landline)		
	Cell Phone(s) Expenses		
	Other Misc. Techno. Fees		

	Cable & Internet		
	Vehicle(s) Payments		
	Vehicle Insurance(s)		
	Gasoline & Servicing		
	Child Care		
	Clothing Expenses		
	Groceries, Snacks/Drinks		
	Eating Out & Starbucks		
	Alcohol, Cold Drinks, Beverages		
	Entertainment, Vacations		
	Misc. Expenses		
	Special Expenses		
	Donations Cash/Non-Cash		
	Life Insurance		
	Medical Insurance		
	Dental Expenses		
	Prescription Costs/Co-Pays		
	Eye Exams & Glasses		
	Federal Taxes		
	State Taxes		

MY MONTHLY INCOME:		**MY TOTAL MONTHLY COSTS:**	**MONTHLY DIFFERENCE:**

Look at the *difference* between your income for the month and your total monthly expenses. Hopefully it is in the black---a positive amount, to be placed into your saving account.

If it is in the "red" and your income does NOT cover your regular monthly expenses, then you need to make some cuts . . . and live within your means.

And you need to do this NOW . . . today! This is critical! It won't go away. You need to balance that budget by being financially proactive!

Make additional copies of budget chart and update it every month.

RECOMMENDATIONS: To balance your budget, you need to look at *all* options. Everything is on the table. For housing, if you're single, consider a roommate to share expenses. If you're married, consider downsizing your home.

If single or married, consider owning/driving only one vehicle (with low mileage), move closer to your job, skip those Starbuck lattes, cook your own meals at home, brown bag it to work, and use only one credit card (pay off the total balance each month).

MORE RECOMMENDATIONS: If you can't pay cash for something, don't buy it. (Save up for it and then buy it when you have the cash.)

Read on for more suggestions to help you in your budgeting process and recommendations to reduce expenses.

HOUSING

You may live in an apartment, in a condo, or a single-family house. You may pay rent or make a mortgage payment each month, along with taxes, insurance, utilities, etc.

Whatever your situation, your *total* "housing" monthly cost should be approximately 20% of your "net" income or "take home pay."

That is, if your "net" income is $1,000 a month, then you should be paying $200 or less per month for your housing ($1,000 X .20 = $200).

Or, if your "net" income is $5,000 a month, then you should be paying $1,000 or less per month.

HOUSING EXPENSES

YOUR MONTHLY "NET" (TAKE-HOME) INCOME	YOUR TOTAL MONTHLY HOUSING EXPENSES
$1,000	$200
$2,000	$400
$5,000	$1,000
$10,000	$2,000
$15,000	$3,000

Please note that I am talking about your TOTAL housing costs. This means, for example if you're a home owner, you need to include *ALL* costs, including your monthly costs for taxes, utilities (garbage, water, lights & gas), home or renters insurance, life insurance, mortgage insurance (to cover your mortgage if you should pass away, to pay off the house so it is free and clear), plus any other housing-related expenses dealing with your home.

Are you paying more than 20% at this time? Can you afford to stay in this situation or are you going deeper and deeper into debt? If so, then you may need to immediately change your situation.

AS A RENTER:

As a renter, you will have your monthly rent to pay, along with any costs for garbage, water, and other utilities, such as gas and electric. You definitely should make a monthly payment towards "renters insurance" to protect you against your loss of your worldly possessions. In addition, there may be other renter costs.

You need to itemize these costs and that total should not exceed 20% of your monthly "take home pay."

If you are renting, you may need to find another apartment or living situation where you pay 20% *or less* of your monthly net income or take home pay. Married or single, consider sharing housing expenses with one or more other people. A studio apartment? A room with kitchen privileges?

RECOMMENDATIONS to renters: By all means, if you are a renter and *can afford ALL the costs involved* in the owning your own home, do purchase one (if you can *really* afford it, using the 20% of net pay criteria). If you can make a 20% down payment (cash) and if you do purchase a home, make sure that you get a "fixed" interest rate and shop around for the lowest interest rate possible. You have been paying rent. Let the rent payment "pay off your house" (and cover all housing-related expenses).

AS A HOME OWNER:

As a homeowner, you have your monthly mortgage payment (unless your home is paid off!), along with the other costs, such as property taxes, insurance (fire, theft, liability, earthquake, etc.), possible association fees, along with any costs for garbage, water, and other utilities, such as gas and electric.

It is important that you itemize all housing-associated costs and that total should not exceed 20% of your monthly "take home pay."

If you are buying your home and *can't afford the total costs involved*, then you may need to sell your home and get into a cheaper housing situation (a rental or cheaper home purchase).

RECOMMENDATIONS to reduce expenses: Share expenses with another family or family members. Move. Choose a different housing situation. Sell the house if it is too expensive for you. Get into a cheaper apartment or condo.

Please note that the 20% rule for housing is conservative, but it should go a long way to keep you "living within your means." (Larger percentages could place you in financial jeopardy or run you into bankruptcy.)

Housing takes a major chunk of your paycheck. It is important to bring this cost within your means.

INVESTMENTS &
"PAYING YOURSELF FIRST"

(10% OF GROSS INCOME)

It is critical to "pay yourself first."

Yes, that's right. One rule of thumb is to have 10% taken out of your check, before you even see it, and then live off the rest. (Sign up at the personnel office where you work to have money directly deposited into a 403(b), 401(k), or other program.) Doing this is the mark of a responsible, mature person.

You need to invest each and every year until retirement. Seek out the advice of a reputable financial advisor.

Read finance books and materials. Educate yourself.

One excellent book list can be found on http://www.bobbrinker.com/books.asp. [This is the web site of Bob Brinker, for financial and retirement planning.] One excellent resource is **Bogle on Mutual Funds: New Perspectives for the Intelligent Investor** by John C. Bogle. Another is **All About Index Funds** by Richard A. Ferri.

You need to be financially secure in retirement, to live comfortably and feel at ease and unworried about your finances and your retirement. There are lots of things you can do *NOW* to ensure your financial future.

Take full advantage of any 403(b) or 401(k) retirement programs, traditional and Roth IRA's, etc. "Full" means to "max" them out, up the greatest amount allowable by law.

Someone who invests $2000 each and every year starting in his/her early-20's will be a millionaire in retirement years, assuming a 10% annual return, no withdrawals are taken, and investments are in tax-deferred accounts.

Social Security is meant to supplement, not be the entire retirement program. You need to save, manage, and build your retirement plan to supplement Social Security. Otherwise, you may not have enough to live on in your retirement years.

Educate yourself about investments and diversified investment programs. Buy bonds, invest in no-load mutual funds, and diversify your investments.

RECOMMENDATIONS for investments: Through the years, people have invested in their homes, buying and paying off the home before retirement. People have also purchased no-load equities (stock market/mutual funds which have on fees upon initial purchase) and "fixed" (bonds, Treasuries, no-load mutual funds, etc.) investments . . . maintaining a "balanced" portfolio (50% in equities/50% in fixed, for example) . . . to supplement Social Security retirement income. I recommend this strategy.

CREDIT CARDS

If you have more than two credit cards, **choose two** of the cards---the ones with the lowest interest rate charges and the ones that give you cash back rewards. (Call the credit card companies and negotiate lower interest rates.)

Cut up the other cards; pay them off as soon as possible.

Use ONE credit card for all your monthly purchases. Use the second credit card for one small purchase each month to keep it active. Remember to pay both of the balances due at the end of the month.

If you lose one card or something happens to it, you have a back-up card (the second one) to use.

If you have **credit card debt** that you cannot pay off at the end of the month, then it is important to pay down that debt each month. Pay as much as you can! Don't just pay the minimum payment. If you only pay the minimum payment, it could take *years* to pay the debt off. You may even end up paying more than double the cost of any one item. It's not worth it.

If you have no carryover credit card debt, good for you!

Important: Pay off your credit card(s) at the end of each and every month. And pay them on time or you will be hit with a huge charge or fine, upwards to $75 and your interest rates will probably be raised and your credit score hurt.

Other than your home or vehicle needed to travel to and from work, *if you can't pay cash for something, don't buy it.*

After you have paid off your credit card debt, then you can start saving towards that one "special purchase" you want. When you have the cash, then buy it. Then you can start saving towards another "special purchase."

Special note: If you are a married couple, both of you should use the SAME credit card/number. He has the card/number in his name and she has the same card/number in her name. This is simpler and it helps with the coordinated family budgeting process. It'll be one monthly bill to pay off. (Use this strategy for multiple members in a "family unit.")

SPECIAL NOTE TO COUPLES: Talk to your credit card company, to ensure that both people are building a credit rating and history.

RECOMMENDATIONS to reduce costs: Use only one credit card and fully pay it off each month. If you can't pay cash for something that month, don't buy it. Save towards it and buy it when you have the cash.

COMMUNICATON SERVICES
(Phones, Internet & Other
Technology Services.)

PHONES: LANDLINE & CELL:

Traditionally, people have had one telephone---a "landline" is as it is now called. It is attached to a telephone line, on land, hence the name "landline."

A cell phone is different---it's wireless. Today, cell phones come in many shapes and sizes, with a wide variety of other services and features.

One landline phone connection could cost about $35 per month in basic charges. One cell phone connection could cost about $75 a month, depending on the additional services and features.

Some people are choosing to drop the landline phone and use only their cell phones. This is cheaper than using both.

However, if cell phone service is down or not functioning, which does happen, landline phones will probably be up and functioning. It's a safety issue. Some people are choosing to keep both, as a result.

Regardless of what services you choose, please note the costs and include in your written monthly budget.

RECOMMENDATIONS to reduce costs: Select the simplest and cheapest of services. Simplicity is paramount. Cheapest is paramount.

You just need basic communication services. You do not *"need"* the latest and every possible "gadget." You do need to be practical and balance your budget. Of course, if your lifestyle permits, the landline phone is usually the most economical.

INTERNET & OTHER TECHNOLOGY SERVICES:

There are various means to obtain Internet services, with various costs involved. Internet services provide a wide range of "speeds" and quality of service. In today's society, the Internet is important and almost a requirement.

It is recommended that you shop around and get the cheapest Internet service available, considering the level of your required tech support, plus usage and speed needs.

Notice the operative word: "need" (necessity, obligation, requirement), as opposed to "want" or "desired" (wish, demand, longing, yearning, fancy, craving, hankering).

When making choices, do make practical decisions, and balance your budget. The same goes for the wide variety of other technology services also available out there.

RECOMMENDATIONS to reduce expenses: Have only one landline into your home. (This is less expensive than two or more lines.) Yes, you can share phone time. For your cell phone, get the cheaper family plan with limited hours (and use for emergency only and family communications only). Skip the "extra" services, which cost more money. You only need to communicate with family. Period. If your child "wants" more phone services or hours (costly!), let him or her get a job and pay for those extras. Shop around for the basic phone and phone service. Some companies offer free basic cell phones if you sign up with them. (No you don't "need" fancy phones!) We're talking practicality here!

TRANSPORTATION

Transportation costs involve vehicle payments, insurance, gasoline costs, servicing expenditures and other transportation costs.

Many people have over-extended themselves by purchasing (and making monthly payments; not paying with cash) one or more expensive vehicles.

Expensive vehicles are often purchased for status symbols instead of viewed as meeting basic transportation needs. More often than not, people with expensive vehicles can be financially strapped or "over-extended" (a euphemism for spending themselves into the poor house).

When asked what their transportation costs are, often only the monthly payment is discussed. Not accurate. You need to include all transportation-related costs, including monthly payments, insurance, gas, servicing costs, tire replacements, mileage, any right-offs, etc.

Many people have several vehicles, for different "needs." This is expensive and in many cases too costly for their budgets. Besides, each person can only drive one car at a time, and each person can chose one multi-functional, practical vehicle, as appropriate.

RECOMMENDATIONS to reduce expenses: Sell the "extra vehicles" and trade in the expensive car (unless it is paid off), for a more practical, less expensive car, especially one with good gas mileage. Car pool. Plan your shopping trips ahead of time, with a list. Do several errands in one trip. Take public transit. Buy on-line to save transportation costs.

CHILDCARE

Childcare is expensive, depending on the services chosen. I've heard mothers lament that childcare costs take a big chunk out of their take home pay.

Reality is: If children are not in school and if the parent or parents aren't at home, then childcare is necessary.

Regardless of the cost, if childcare is necessary, then include childcare in your monthly budget. To balance your monthly budget, make cuts elsewhere, downsize elsewhere.

To reduce childcare expenses, consider having one parent stay home to provide childcare. Or one parent might work part time while children are in school. Or parents of several families must work together to share their childcare responsibilities. Or perhaps extended family members could help out, and sometimes there are special programs to help working parents.

Do the math. Sometimes it is cost-effective for one parent to stay at home. Maybe the parent can increase the family income by providing childcare services for their neighbors and family or finding employment that allows the parent to work from home. It depends on the level of income as compared to childcare and other work-related expenses.

RECOMMENDATIONS to decrease expenses: Research childcare options and after-school programs. Some are less expensive than others. Move closer to your job(s). Share childcare with other families in the neighborhood. Work part-time or work from home. Look into volunteering to "match" costs of childcare (volunteering sometimes offsets fees). Invite an older family member or friend to live with you, sharing some of the expenses in exchange for providing childcare.

CLOTHING

Clothing is a normal budget expense. Some people make it a major expense. That's well and good, if you can afford it.

Clothing is an area in which you can save substantial money, if it is a big expense now.

Clothing requirements vary, depending on your job, but regardless of your job, clothing expenses do NOT have to be expensive or excessive.

Your wardrobe requirements should be planned, deliberate, and practical. No impulse buying,
just the basics and no "fads."

You *CAN* get along with a few basic outfits. And these basic outfits can be very stylish too!

After making out your monthly budget (and if it is in the black and includes the 10% allocation of your gross income to investments), decide what you can practically afford for clothing and then stick to that amount each month. Then do not exceed that amount!

If you can't afford to allocate any money for clothes then don't spend anything on clothes. Period.

RECOMMENDATIONS to decrease expenses: Shop thrift shops for anything you desperately need. Or do without. Save up cash to pay for something you desperately need.

FOOD: GROCERIES,
SNACKS & EATING OUT

Good, nutritional food is necessary and critical for survival. Basic food is necessary. So is clean, fresh water.

Eating out or purchasing pre-cooked or prepared meals comes with a big price. Such foods, more often than not, have poor ingredients (many with non-nutritional chemicals) and high prep costs.

However, in today's world, people often believe that we "need" more expensive, prepared or packaged (and chemical-laden) foods or drinks to survive. Not true.

Most people spend too much "eating out" which is another way of saying . . . We are rich enough to hire a private cook to prepare our food, so we don't have to cook. (Are you THAT rich?)

When you "eat out" at an expensive restaurant or go fast food, you are paying a chef or cook to prepare it for you.

If you buy a frozen dinner, you are hiring someone to prepare the meal for you.

Are you rich enough for your own private chef?
Probably not.

Save money. Cook at home, preferably from scratch. Eat at home, all three meals. (And don't use prepared or packaged meals either.) Some people who eat out several times a week have found that their food budget can be cut almost in half by "eating in," not to mention the quality control you bring to the kitchen.

Don't know how to cook? Learn. Read recipes in cookbooks. Ask your older friends and family members to teach you. Some of my favorite standby cookbooks are the **Better Homes and Gardens Cookbook, The Betty Crocker Cookbook,** and **The Joy of Cooking**.

Buy fresh organic in-season vegetables and fruits from local farmer's markets and vegetable stands. (These are usually delicious and lower in cost.)

Buy the basics, not junk food or non-nutritional snacks or drinks. Too expensive (and not good for you either). If you don't have them in the house, you can't eat them. Plus, you'll save money!

Make out weekly menus for all three meals. Make double batches of meals and then alternate meals. Cook a double meatloaf. Serve on Monday and Wednesday, for example. Make a large casserole. Serve on Tuesday and Thursday.

Eat before you go shopping, so you are not hungry. Make out your shopping list, making sure you have all needed items for your planned weekly menus. Then, ONLY buy what is on your shopping list. No impulse buying. No junk food. No packaged snacks (make them at home). No sugary drinks (Pepsi, Coke, etc.).

Forget the $5 per cup coffee houses and make your own coffee at home and take to work.

RECOMMENDATIONS to decrease food costs: Purchase only basic food needs, and fresh in-season fruits and vegetables. Collect and use store coupons. Don't purchase junk food, pre-prepared or frozen meals or sugary/non-nutritional drinks. Don't eat out. Cook at home, all three meals and brown bag it for lunch. Shop only for items on your shopping list. Watch the ads, buy on sale, and plan your weekly meals around sale items and in-season fruits and vegetables. Buy in bulk where possible, as bulk is usually cheaper.

ENTERTAINMENT

Entertainment (along with costs of baby sitting, eating out, tickets, etc.) is wonderful for those with an adequate budget. However, for those with budget problems, it is not so wonderful.

Everyone likes "entertainment." However, in today's world, the expectations have overrun and overwhelmed our budgets. It has gone beyond reason.

We do not "need" to spend money on entertainment, for example video rentals. We do not "need" to go to that concert, play, or movie. We do not "need" to have that expensive theatre popcorn, candy or drinks. We do not "need" to have that DVD or CD or entertainment center. These are all extras . . . niceties, if you have the money; however, if you do not have a balanced budget or if money is tight, then just don't buy any of these. Period. None. Don't go out. Don't spend money. Postpone such niceties until your budget is balanced.

There are many "freer" options, just look around, be proactive and creative. Use your imagination.

Stay home. Play board games. Watch TV. Read a good book. (Free books at the library!)

Write a book---your life's story. Bake a cake. Play a card game. Telephone a friend (local call!). Write a letter. Work on that special project. Reorganize your desk and files. Take a nap. Give yourself a pedicure or manicure. Take a walk around the local park. Walk the dog. Visit a friend. Meditate. Do Yoga. Jog. There are endless ideas our there!

MISC. EXPENSES

This section of your monthly budget is for any misc. expenses.

You may choose to list a set amount each month, for those small extras, not accounted for in the budget.

<u>RECOMMENDATION</u>: Keep track of each and every expenditure, no matter how small. (Carry a pen and small pad with you at all times and record each expenditure. Keep all receipts.) Compare the actual total monthly misc. expenses with what you have allocated. If you go over budget in misc. expenses, then you need to re-evaluate your budget and your misc. expenditures. Something needs to change.

There's an old saying, "Watch your pennies and the dollars will take care of themselves." It's true. Be very cautious of spending even the smallest of amounts. It's a mindset. I'm not saying to NOT spend money. I'm saying be cautious and conservative. Spend only if it is a real emergency or a necessary basic. Don't spend because "you want it."

If you find that your "misc. expenses" tend to be large, then they are not small incidentals. They need to be allocated each month in your

budget. (Remember, you need to keep that budget balanced and in the black!)

Develop a good mindset in finances! And keep those misc. expenses "low."

SPECIAL EXPENSES

This section of your monthly budget is for any and all "special" or unique expenses not listed elsewhere in your budget.

A special expense may be for a specific purchase, event or person.

Whatever it is, it can be listed in your monthly budget.

You may need to save each month towards that special expense, to have the money ready (cash in your savings account) when you need to pay for it.

You may have as many special expenses . . . that you can afford, if it fits into your budget.

You may write each "special expense" on a separate line of your monthly budget chart. (There are numerous blank lines for your convenience for this purpose.)

DONATIONS

It long has been a rule of thumb to donate upwards to 10% of your income to church and/or charities of your choice. (At church, it is called "tithing.")

To determine what 10% of your monthly income is, just multiple .10 times your total monthly income.

For example, if you make $1,500 a month [$1,500 times .10 equals $150], that means that you will allocate $150 each month for donations.

If you donate to charities recognized by the federal government as non-profit charitable organizations, then your donations are deductible.

If you donate to your church, synagogue, or other recognized religious organizations, etc., your deductions are deductible too.

You need to clarify eligible deductions with your tax consultant, just to make sure of your own personal allowable deductions.

INSURANCES

You need to allocate each month towards several types of insurances. All of these are necessary and you should not shortchange your insurance needs. You need to consult with your insurance agent(s) as to your own personal specific needs.

Please note that many insurance companies will automatically deduct monthly premiums out of your check, before you even see your check. This is a highly recommended procedure. Have your insurances automatically deducted each month. Then you know they are paid and you are covered.

LIFE INSURANCE: If you have a family, you need to provide for them if something happens to you. In my opinion, the face value of the insurance amount should at least cover paying off your home and provide for one year of income for the family.

Take out "term" insurance. There are other types of plans out there, but they are more like "investments" (which will cost you more). Just get the basic insurance: "term" insurance. It goes for a specific term or length of time and pays off only if you pass away during that time period.

You need to apply for life insurance earlier in your life, when you are younger. You'll more likely to be healthy and it'll be cheaper.

MEDICAL INSURANCE: This is a big and important item. Medical insurance coverage needs to be included in your monthly budget. Reduce other areas of the budget to make this happen. Don't neglect this necessary and important expense. (Large medical bills not covered by medical insurance are a frequent reason for bankruptcy.)

Medical premiums vary, depending on coverage
(what is paid for by the insurance company and how much of it is covered). Often people are required to pay "co-pays" for office calls ($25, for example, paid by you out-of-pocket, and the insurance company paying the rest of the cost, up to the policy limit). Often people are required to pay a "deductible" ($100 paid by you out-of-pocket with the insurance company paying the rest of the cost, up to the policy limit). Do some serious comparison-shopping for the appropriate coverage for you and your family.

DENTAL INSURANCE: Dental insurance covers teeth cleanings, dental work, and, depending on your coverage, orthodontia work you or your family members may need. It is common to have only about $2,000 a year per person for cleanings and dental work, with optional orthodontia coverage (for an additional premium). These premiums tend to be reasonable, but you need to weigh the necessity and premium costs.

It should be noted that the medical community has found that dental health is important to your overall general health.

VISION INSURANCE: Vision insurance often covers an annual eye exam, new frames and lenses every two years and some payment towards contacts (in lieu of traditional lenses and frames). Check with your insurance agent regarding coverage options and premium costs, which you will have to weigh.

DISABILITY INSURANCE:

If you are working, then you need to consider insurance for if/when you become disabled and cannot work. You need to guarantee your income for you and/or your family. If you become too injured to work, for example, and it is not a job related injury, then disability insurance could help you during the time you cannot work---to help maintain your standard of living.

LONG TERM CARE INSURANCE:

If, during your retirement years, you cannot care for yourself, long term care insurance can help pay for needed home/health care or assisted-living care, not covered by Medicare or regular medical insurance programs.

It is recommended that you begin early, at a younger age, to obtain this insurance. The younger you are when you take it out, the lower the premiums. Plus, you never know when you will need this type of care. Most people assume it will happen after retirement age, but it could be sooner.

VEHICLE INSURANCE: For each vehicle or watercraft you own, you need to have at least the minimum insurance, as per your state law.

It is recommended that you carry more than minimum legal requirement: $100,000 per person for bodily injury; $25,000 property damage per accident; $25,000 medical insurance per person; comprehensive coverage; emergency road service; car rental and travel expenses per accident; uninsured motor vehicle property damage; and $10,000 for your death, dismember and loss of sight.

If you select a deductible, example $1000, then your premiums may be less. If something happens, however, you have to pay the deductible out of your own pocket and the insurance company will cover the rest.

PROPERTY & LIABILITY INSURANCE: If you own a home, you need *homeowner's insurance* to cover your home and property, plus personal liability coverage (in case someone sues you).

It is recommended that you have your home appraised to ensure that you have the appropriate level of home (dwelling) coverage and dwelling extensions (unattached garage, pool house, etc.)

It is recommended that you get coverage for actual dwelling replacement; personal property coverage (about 70% of dwelling cost?); loss of use (actual expenses incurred); personal liability ($300,000?); damage to property of others ($500?); and medical payments to others ($5,000?), with a deductible ($1,000 or $2,000?). (It needs to be noted at additional coverage tends to be minimal in cost---not that much more.)

You can obtain discounts on your premium for a home alert system, for insuring multi-vehicles, claim free, etc. (Ask about these.)

Study carefully the so-called *replacement clause*. You need to have actual replacement at today's cost. Sometimes things are replaced at current market value. Things are "depreciated" in value and you get little for older items. If you paid $600 for that TV five years ago and it'll cost $1000 to replace today, the insurance company could give you what it would cost today to replace it ($1,000) or the insurance company could "depreciate" it and give you only $100 (today's value). Just remember that you do pay more in premium cost for the actual replacement at today's cost. You get what you pay for . . .

If you rent, then you need *renter's insurance* (to cover the contents of your home), plus liability insurance (in case someone sues you).

Again, check your replacement clause carefully. Make sure you see it in writing. (Verbal descriptions from your insurance agent do not count.)

As part of property & liability coverage, special coverage may need to be obtained for **FLOOD, HURRICANE, TORNATO** and other such events.

EARTHQUAKE INSURANACE: You need earthquake insurance if you live in an area prone to having earthquakes.

It is recommended that you have this insurance if you live in an area prone to having earthquakes (or within 250 miles of an area prone to having earthquakes---just to be safe).

You need to get insurance for your home (dwelling), any other buildings adjacent to your home (extensions to the dwelling), loss of personal property, and loss of use.

Many policies require a large deductible, sometimes 15%. That is, if an earthquake damages your home, etc., you have to pay the first 15% of the cost of the total damages, and then the insurance company pays the rest, up to the limits noted on your insurance coverage. Most importantly, ou need to have your home, etc. valued at its current value and keep that value updated each year. (Many people pay less of a premium, but they get less coverage.)

UMBRELLA INSURANCE: "Umbrella" insurance is a personal liability program and a supplement to all your other insurances. (I recommend at least $2 million coverage, in addition to your home or renter's insurance coverage.)

Consult with your insurance agent about the cost of obtaining additional coverage, additional $ millions, as it usually does not cost that much more.

MONTHLY INSURANCE COSTS:

Please note what you annually pay for all your insurances, divide that number by 12 [months] and you will get your monthly insurance costs. Then, include the insurance costs in your monthly budget.

ESTABLISHING YOUR INSURANCE NEEDS:

Talk with your insurance agent(s) about the various options and coverage. Look at all options and decide what is best for you and your family. But do not skip basic insurance coverage. Be serious and careful in this area.

If the time should ever come and you are subjected to a loss of some sort, you will be glad you were protected.

Cut your budget elsewhere to ensure appropriate insurance coverage. It's important.

TAXES

There's an old saying that nothing is certain except death and taxes. True. You will have to include several taxes in your monthly budget.

HOME TAXES: If you pay your home tax, for example, once a year (in one installment) or twice a year (in two installments), you should divide you yearly home tax amount by 12 (for 12 months) and include it in your monthly budget.

However, if you already have a mortgage, the home taxes may be included in your monthly home payment plan along with the required home insurance. (You need to check on this, just to make sure.)

FEDERAL INCOME TAXES: You will be paying taxes to the federal government.

If you take home a paycheck, you will have a certain amount taken out of your check. If you have too much taken out, you will receive a refund. If you have too little taken out, you will have to pay a lump sum to the federal government, with a possible fine under certain circumstances. (Confer with your tax consultant regarding how much to have withheld from your paycheck.)

Under certain circumstances, you may need to pay an additional amount for federal taxes due in April for the prior fiscal year. Divide that amount by 12 months and include in your monthly budget, so you have the money in April when it is due and payable. (Save ahead of time.)

STATE INCOME TAXES: You MAY be paying taxes to your state government, albeit, some states do not have income taxes.

If you do have to pay state taxes and you take home a paycheck, you will have state taxes taken out of your paycheck.

Again, if you have too much taken out, you will receive a refund. If you have too little taken out, you will have to pay a lump sum to the state government, with a possible fine under certain circumstances. (Confer with your tax consultant regarding how much to have withheld from your paycheck.)

Under certain circumstances, you may need to pay an additional amount for state taxes due in April for the prior fiscal year. Divide that amount by 12 months and include in your monthly budget, so you have the money in April when it is due and payable. (Save ahead of time.) Refer to your last year's tax bill or statement as a guide.

OTHER MISC. TAXES: Depending on where you live, you may have to pay other types of taxes. Do plan on these, saving ahead of time, so you have the cash to pay the taxes when due and payable.

PLANNING AHEAD
(YOUR 5-YEAR PROJECTION PLAN)

If you *REALLY* want to be financially prudent, mature, and responsible, you will plan ahead. That means you save ahead . . . and have the cash on hand (in the savings account) to pay that anticipated bill when it is due and payable.

Some people have what is called their **"5-Year Plan."** They look ahead. They write down any big-bill items that will have to be paid in future years. Then they divide that amount by the number of years and then divide by 12 months, and add that to their monthly budget. They save that amount each month. They deposit that amount each month in their FDIC-protected savings account. Then, when that big bill comes up, the money is there.

Let's take an example: A new roof for the older home you own. Let's say that roof will cost $10,000 and you expect to need a new roof in five years. Divide the $10,000 by five [years] and then by 12 [months], to get the $167 monthly allocation. Then, list the new roof as a "special expense" in your monthly budget and allocate $167 to be saved each month.

Prudent people plan ahead and allocate, as necessary, for larger items, such as replacement of kitchen appliances, painting of home, orthodontia needs for young children, future college tuition and books, etc.

In addition to budget items discussed in other parts of this book, here is a list of some items (as examples) you may need to plan for in your monthly budget and your "5-Year Plan":

- Replacement of kitchen appliances
- Replacement of home air conditioner/heating unit
- Painting of exterior of home
- Painting of interior of home
- Replacement of roof
- Windows replacement
- Automobile replacement
- New furniture
- New electronic equipment
- College expenses
- Orthodontia work
- Future wedding expenses
- Special travel plans

Do you have your "5-Year Plan" in place? You should. You will be glad if you do.

A SUMMARY OF RECOMMENDATIONS FOR BUDGET CUTS & INVESTMENTS

Throughout this book, there have been suggestions for budget cuts and investments. To assist the reader, those suggestions are summarized here for the reader's review and consideration.

BUDGETS:

To balance your budget, you need to look at *all* options. Everything is on the table. For housing, if you're single, consider a roommate to share expenses. If you're married, consider downsizing your home.

If single or married, consider owning/driving only one vehicle (with low mileage), move closer to your job, skip those Starbuck lattes, cook your own meals at home, brown bag it to work, and use only one credit card (pay off the total balance each month).

If you can't pay cash for something, don't buy it. (Save up for it and then buy it when you have the cash.)

HOUSING:

If you are **renting**, you may need to find another apartment or living situation where you pay 20% *or less* of your monthly net income or take home pay. Married or single, consider sharing housing expenses with one or more other people. A studio apartment? A room with kitchen privileges?

RENTERS: By all means, if you are a renter and can afford ALL the costs involved in the owning your own home, do purchase one (if you can *really* afford it, using the 20% of net pay criteria). If you do purchase a home, make sure that you get a "fixed" interest rate and shop around for the lowest interest rate possible. You have been paying rent. Let the rent payment "pay off your house" (and cover all housing-related expenses). To possibly save thousands of dollars on your mortgage or re-financing (and dodge those financing pitfalls), check out *Mortgage Rip-Offs and Money Savers* by Carolyn Warren.

HOME BUYERS: If you are buying your home, then you may need to sell your home and get into a cheaper housing situation (rental or cheaper home purchase).

Share expenses with another family or family members. Move. Choose a different housing situation. Sell the house if it is too expensive for you. Get into a cheaper apartment or condo. Rent instead of buying? Shared housing?

INVESTMENTS:

Through the years, people have invested in their homes, buying and paying off the home before retirement. People have also purchased no-load equities (stock market/mutual funds which have on fees upon initial purchase) and "fixed" (bonds, Treasuries, no-load mutual funds, etc.) investments . . . maintaining a "balanced" portfolio (50% in equities/50% in fixed, for example) . . . to supplement Social Security retirement income. I recommend a balanced portfolio, especially as you get within ten years of retirement.

CERDIT CARDS:

Use only one credit card and fully pay it off each month. If you can't pay cash for something that month, don't buy it. Save towards it and buy it when you have the cash.

COMMUNICATION SERICES:

Select the simplest and cheapest of services. Simplicity is paramount. Cheapest is paramount. You just need basic communication services. You do not *"need"* the latest and every possible "gadget." You do need to be practical and balance your budget.

Have only one landline into your home. (This is less expensive than two or more lines.) Yes, you can share phone time. (You won't die, I promise you.) For your cell phone, get the cheaper family plan with limited hours (and use for emergency only and family communications only). Skip the "extra" services, which cost more money. You only need to communicate with family. Period. If your child "wants" more phone services or hours (costly!), let him or her get a job and pay for those extras. Shop around for the basic phone and phone service. Some companies offer free basic cell phones if you sign up with them. (No you don't "need" fancy phones!) We're talking practicality here!

TRANSPORTATION:

Sell the "extra vehicles" and trade in the expensive car (unless it is paid off), for a more practical, less expensive car, especially one with good gas mileage. Car pool. Plan your shopping trips ahead of time, with a list. Do several errands in one trip. Take public transit. Buy on-line to save transportation costs.

CHILDCARE:

Research childcare options and after-school programs. Some are less expensive than others. Move closer to your job(s). Share childcare with other families in the neighborhood. Work part-time or work from home. Look into volunteering to "match" costs of childcare (volunteering sometimes offsets fees). Invite an older family member or friend to live with you, sharing some of the expenses in exchange for providing childcare.

CLOTHING:

Shop thrift shops for anything you desperately need. Or do without. Save up cash to pay for something you desperately need. Sell or place on consignment any extra good clothing you have or haven't worn in

the last year. Donate your extra clothing (and consult your tax consultant about taking the deductions).

Your closet should not be bulging. If it is, you have over-spent. Most people only wear a few of the items in their closet and the rest is just taking up space. (The rule of thumb is to donate or sell what you have not worn in the last year.)

FOOD-Groceries, Snacks & Eating Out:

Purchase only basic food needs, and fresh in-season fruits and vegetables. Collect and use store coupons. Don't purchase junk food, pre-prepared or frozen meals or sugary/non-nutritional drinks. Don't eat out. Cook at home, all three meals. Shop only for items on your shopping list. Brown bag it to school, work, etc. Watch the ads, buy on sale, and plan your weekly meals around sale items and in-season fruits and vegetables. Buy in bulk where possible (if cheaper).

ENTERTAINMENT:

Stay home. Play board games. Watch TV. Read a good book. (Free books at the library!) Write a book---your life's story. Bake a cake. Play a card game. Telephone a friend (local call!). Write a letter. Work on that special project. Reorganize your desk and files. Take a nap. Give yourself a pedicure or manicure. Take a walk around the local park. Walk the dog. Visit a friend. Meditate. Do Yoga. Jog. There are endless ideas our there!

POLITICALLY-INCORRECT COMMENTS

During the writing process of this book, several "politically-incorrect" comments popped into this author's mind. For some inexplicable reason, this author feels compelled to share these comments with the reader.

These comments were intended to be of "HELP" in the reader's financial thinking process . . . not as negative personal comments on the reader himself or herself. Please take the comments in the manner in which they are given.

If you elect to do so, read through these comments, select those that apply and ignore those that do not apply to you the reader.

Remember, this author has included these comments for you the reader, partly in humor but partly in seriousness.

FINANCIAL PRIORITIES:

As a parent, do you spend money on a fancy, expensive sports car while neglecting your young child's dental needs? *(This says that you think your personal need for a "thing" is more important than caring for your child.)*

As a husband, do you spend money on special sport shoes and ignore your wife's plea for grocery money? *(This says that your think your need for "things" are more important than feeding your family.)*

As a wife, do you routinely overspend your monthly budget? *(This says that you lack self-control. It says that you really don't care about providing for your family.)*

As a family-provider, do you spend money eating out but do not provide for your own life insurance? *(This says that you'd rather have that eating luxury than provide for your family's future financial security. Should you unexpectedly pass away, your temporary enjoyment could result in thrusting your family into desperate poverty.*

You'd rather have them in live in desperate poverty if you pass away, so you can have this temporary enjoyment.)

As a teenager, do you spend money on things that you know you really can't afford? Hair stylists? Manicure and pedicures? Designer clothing? Expensive jewelry? Trips? Expensive homes? Video and electronic equipment? *(That says you don't care about you or your family's financial future. You place their future in jeopardy, because you cannot say no to yourself.)*

HOUSING:

Housing takes a major chunk of your paycheck. Just make sure it only takes about 20% or less of your monthly "net" or take home pay. *(If you don't, then you, more than likely, will not be able act in a responsible manner.)*

Yes, that's right. One rule of thumb is to have 10% taken out of your check (by your employer or by yourself if you are self-employed), before you even see it, and then live off the rest. *(Doing this is the mark of a responsible, wise person*

CHILDCARE:

Children, even teens, should not be left at home alone, unsupervised without a responsible adult. Bad things can happen when children, even teens, are unsupervised.

Some people believe that children, even teens, can be left unsupervised, or sent to a mall to "hang out," or left at school for hours on the unsupervised playground. This is not true and even dangerous. I believe it is child neglect and child abandonment. Period.

It is the parents' legal and moral responsibility to provide for the care and supervision of all of their children. Children need a roof over their heads, basic food and clothing, and lots of structure and love. (They do not "need" big houses, expensive cars, costly foods & snacks, designer clothes, expensive electronics, etc. . . and neither do you.)

Sometimes one parent must stay home to provide childcare. Or one parent must work part time while children are in school. Or parents of several families must work together to share their childcare responsibilities. Or extended

family members need to help out. Sometimes there are special programs to help working parents.

Parents, do the math. Sometimes it is cost-effective for one parent to stay at home. Maybe the parent can increase the family income by providing childcare services for their neighbors and family or finding employment that allows the parent to work from home. It depends on the level of income as compared to childcare and other work-related expenses.

LIVING WITHIN ONE"S MEANS:

If one does not LIVE WITHIN THEIR MEANS, then one could be called irresponsible, negligent, ignorant, selfish, immature, just plain stupid, and a whole host of other bad adjectives. Plus, we'll feel like failures and not too happy with the unpleasant consequences or ourselves.

FINAL COMMENTS

As stated at the beginning, this book was written for anyone in need of additional assistance in doing a family budget, managing their finances and "living within their means." I hope that it has served you well.

It is expected that this budget guide has helped you know the "budgeting process," how to manage your finances, and "live within your means."

It is desired that you now know the answer to that original question: "Can I afford it?"

Yes, you can afford it---if it **IS INCLUDED** in your monthly budget . . . your balanced, accurate monthly budget.

No, you cannot afford it---if it is **NOT** included in your monthly budget . . . your balanced, accurate monthly budget.

This guide was written reflecting the author's experience and opinions as to what constitutes a "good" family budget and how to "live within your means."

The goal of this book is to help you be successful and, therefore, effect your entire life and sense of financial well-being . . . for to you be successful in managing your finances and plan for a comfortable, stable future! I hope this book met its goals.

HERE'S TO YOUR SUCCESSFUL BUDGETING!